Touch The Wind

Creative Worship with Children

Jo Carr

The Upper Room
Nashville

Illustrations by Charla Honea

Scripture quotations are from the Revised Standard Version of
the Bible, copyrighted 1946, 1952 and © 1971 by the Division
of Christian Education of the National Council of Churches of
Christ in the U.S.A., and are used by permission.

"Treat the Earth Kindly," appearing on page 22, reprinted by
permission of The Coca-Cola Company.

"The Sacrament of Fire" by John Oxenham, © 1928 by John
Oxenham, © renewed 1956, Erica Oxenham, is used by
permission of Theo Oxenham.

Library of Congress Catalog Card Number: 74-33831

UR-321-15-0675

TOUCH THE WIND
Creative Worship with Children

Contents

Introduction

This is not a blow-by-blow guidebook to worship, showing *the* sure way to unfold before your child an awareness of the love of God. It is simply an accumulation of suggested possibilities. Browse among them. Some will sound right for you and usable. Use them. Perhaps they will serve to trigger your own creative thinking, and you will come up with ideas that are better because they are uniquely appropriate to your child and your situation.

This is not a suggested program of brainwashing. Do not hammer away at a concept—even a valid one. Neither lecture nor teach, overtly. Just be aware of God in his world and say so, occasionally and simply. Celebrate the beautiful, the unpredictable, the temporary, the daily—*with* your child—and the experience of worship that comes may very well come to you both.

So browse among these pages. They need not be read or done in order. They need not *all* be used. There is no schedule involved here, but some of the suggestions may help you articulate what you would like to say and help you demonstrate in terms a preschooler can understand that *you* know the God of love.

Let there be no uptightness—"I've got to *do* all these dozens of things!" Just relax, and enjoy the creative adventures of worship that lie ahead for you and the child you love. "Words," you say. "Words, words, words. What can we *do*, my child and I, as an act of worship?" Let's begin.

Soliloquy of a Parent

There is a person whom I love. It happens to be a *small* person, still very young in the ways of the world. She—he—is unique, unrepeatable, and wise with the intuitive wisdom of childhood. She is two now—or three or four or five. And very dear to me.

If I could give this beloved child-person a gift—one single splendid gift of anything that is or ever was—I would like most to give this small person a feeling of communion with God—a love, a sense of Presence, an awareness of God's love.

This gift is not, of course, one that I can purchase. Neither is it one that I can *guarantee* for her, however hard I strive.

And yet, there are ways in which I can help this child become aware of the one Giver of all things.

It is the purpose of this small book to investigate some ways of helping the child become more aware of God's love. One does not lecture with great effectiveness to a two-year-old about the nature of God. But one may kneel with a two-year-old to examine a tulip, and one may be stirred as she is with the beauty of it—and one may even say, "Isn't it a wonder, this that God has made?"

It is through such shared experiences that a child comes to know some things about God. He is bountiful and infinitely creative. And he loves us.

How shall I convey *that* to my child—that God loves her? She knows that we love her, for we tell her so and show her so, in a thousand countless daily ways.

So? Maybe this is a clue. Maybe her concept of God's love, too, shall come by the accumulation of small and daily experiences of his bounty.

But I forget.

I forget to *articulate* it, to say, "This is of God!" I can't think of a way to say it, so I let it go unsaid. I can't think of a way to show it, so it goes unshown.

And yet, this is the *one gift* I would like most to give my child.

I shall try, but where do I begin? Are there *little* experiences of worship which I can provide—this week—today? Are there things we can *do,* my child and I, that will help?

1

Reach Out Through Poetry and Music

Enjoy poetry with your child. Read it. Quote it. Remember that endless repetition is delicious to the little child, and quote some things often enough that he can quote them, too.

Quote some poetry just for the lilt and rhythm of it. Quote some because of the gem of a thought it contains. Such a gem, remembered later, warms the heart! One friend of little children put it this way:

> Keep a poem in your pocket,
> And a picture in your head,
> And you'll never be lonely
> At night when you're in bed! [1]

Sing your praise.

> Then sings my soul, my Savior God to thee;
> How great thou art.

> Carl Boberg

Sing as you wash dishes—fun songs and hymns of praise. A hymn learned in childhood is a message-in-song that keeps coming back to the mind all life long.

---

1. Beatrice Schenk de Regniers, *Something Special* (New York: Harcourt, Brace and World, 1958). Reprinted by permission.

Sing easy songs, over and over, until the child knows them without ever having been aware of trying to learn them—and adjust your pitch and tempo to accommodate your child's singing along with you. Sing harder songs—some for learning, some for the joy of listening to, some simply as expression of your own faith, your own joy in living.

Sing carols, all month before Christmas. The message of carols helps such a great deal to keep Christmas in perspective.

> Infant holy, Infant lowly,
> For His bed a cattle stall.
>
> From the Polish
> English words by E. M. G. Reed

And sing that old, gay, hurry-and-see song about children worshiping at the crib of the Christ—"Bring the Torch, Jeannette, Isabella."

To help the child understand what constitutes a gift of love, sing together the story of "The Little Drummer Boy." This song makes sense to a child at three. Then at five, the child can understand and appreciate Christina Rossetti's poem-become-a-carol, "In the Bleak Midwinter." (See page 44.)

Concentrate on a new child-carol every Christmas, until you and the child know it well. Each year, then, you increase your own treasury of carols by one.

Bend a "book-holder-opener" out of a coat hanger, and put it on the windowsill in front of you to hold a hymnal while you wash dishes. Good way to learn a new-to-you song.

Sing "Joy to the World" in July! It is equally appropriate then as an expression of joy.

Sing in the car. Sing together, you and your child, on the way to the bank or the supermarket. Or covet that time of side-by-sideness for talking and listening.

Sing on trips. Carry a hymnal in the glove compartment of the car, and learn a *new* hymn as the miles go by.

Burst into appropriate song to express the mood of the moment:

"O Beautiful for Spacious Skies"
"Awake, Awake, To Love and Work"
"Oh, What a Beautiful Morning"
"Now the Day Is Over"
"Day Is Dying in the West"

Or sing the old around-the-campfire chorus:

"I See the Moon, the Moon Sees Me."

Include some contemporary songs in your repertoire:

"Bridge Over Troubled Waters"
"We Shall Overcome"
"What the World Needs Now"

Sing "Amazing Grace" movingly. Sing "Bless This House" and "Blessed Be the Tie" and "God Bless America." Sing "Steal Away," and talk about how the song was used during the slavery years to pass the word from field to field that there would be a meeting tonight—a forbidden gathering of the faithful, meeting in secret to worship God. "Steal away to Jesus!"

Sing prayers and praise and messages of love. Don't worry if the sacred laps over into the secular, or the secular into the sacred. Sing "I Love You, a Bushel and a Peck!"

Sing to your child from the first weeks of life, for even an infant enjoys and responds to music. Let there be times when record or radio music provides soft and pleasant background for play. Sing lullabies and nursery songs, gentle music and happy music.

Sing old songs, "Let Us Break Bread Together," and newer ones, "They Will Know We Are Christians by Our Love." And humbly, "How Great Thou Art."

And remember to sing some of them often enough that they become part of the child's own repertoire. What greater legacy can you give a child than such a treasury of music through which to express the heights of personal joys, the depths of individual needs.

Play records. Some children have their own "child-proof" record players and can be free to make music whenever they are inclined to do so. Others can get Mom to "Put on a record for *me.*"

Add a new record to the collection from time to time, remembering that it will be played over and over and over and will become part of the child's own thinking. We might as well make our record choices intentional whether they be sacred or secular. You might want to look for "It's a Small, Small World" and "Getting to Know You," along with some good selections of Christmas carols, perhaps including "Do You Hear What I Hear?" And include some, without words—"Finlandia," perhaps, and the Peer Gynt Suite, from which "Anitra's Dance" and "Morning Song" are delightful expressions of mood as is the more familiar "Hall of the Mountain King." You may wish to look for Pablo Casals's lovely cello arrangement of "Jesu, Joy of Man's Desiring." Or the long-playing record of *Switched-on Bach.*

It does not have to be labeled a children's record or show nursery rhyme people on the cover to be something children will enjoy. You may discover that your child's favorite record is an expressive tone-poem by Antonín Dvořák. He will like Burl Ives's folk music and Franz Liszt's Hungarian dances and may well prefer both to some of the things that are foisted off as "children's" music. Choose some music that is light and gay, to dance and be glad to; some that is calm and restful to dream and unwind to; and some that is rich and moving, that stirs the soul and helps child or adult find expression for the inexpressible. Play records to go to sleep by, occasionally, either at naptime or at night.

Parent as well as child can initiate the putting on of a record—and then parent as well as child can express a reaction to it. *Do* express it. Say, "Oh, that makes me feel like. . . ." What? Yodeling? Dancing? Express with more than words the way the music makes you feel. Waltz to it or sway to it, moving arms and body in unaffected response to the music itself. How a child *loves* this and quickly joins into it, losing all *self*-consciousness in total response.

This is a real and valid way to express and to experience worship. We parents, all tied up in preconceived notions of what worship ought to be, might remind ourselves, "David danced before the Lord with all his might" (2 Sam. 6:14), and the psalmist called the people "to praise his name with dancing" (Psalm 149:3).

So can we—with our children—swaying and turning, lifting our arms up to God and out to each other—enact our praises and express with our whole bodies this moment of worship.

Sometimes there will be a moment when you can join your child in listening to a record. You simply sit down unobtrusively to experience together that moment of "in-tuneness." It isn't necessary to sermonize when the music stops, but once in a while you might express without fanfare a simple prayer, "Thank you God, for such moments."

There will also be times when you will see your child listening, and you will deliberately *not* join in, *not* intrude in that private moment, but go on about your own affairs with a thanksgiving prayer of your own.

Remember the child's right to privacy. Remember the child's need for a certain amount of wholesome neglect.

6

2

Watch Things That Grow

Start a sweet potato vine. Get a sweet potato from a super-market or a fruit stand or a natural foods store. Make sure to buy one that has not been treated to retard sprouting. The traditional method is to choose one that is fat enough not to slip all the way down into a quart jar. Or, you may insert three or four toothpicks into the big end of the sweet potato to keep it from falling in. Fill the jar with enough water to cover the lower portion of the sweet potato, and store it in a dark place. The child will enjoy being allowed to crawl right into a lower cupboard to put it away "way at the back." Leave it in the dark for ten days or two weeks, until roots start. Then place it in a window where it will get plenty of light. Talk about the beauty of God's world and the wonder of growth, as you watch thread-like roots and tiny new curled leaves on the sweet potato vine. In a few months it will grow into a truly handsome houseplant.

Plant a potato eye. Cut a piece of Irish potato, including an eye, that is about a cubic inch in size. Plant it deep in a pot of soil, eye up, and watch it grow. An Irish potato vine is one of the prettiest ever.

Plant birdseed. Birdseed, the ordinary kind that you buy at the pet shop or grocery store to feed the parakeet, is made up of a variety of grass seeds, primarily millet. Because it sprouts so quickly, it is fun for a child to grow. Provide half an egg carton to hold the garden, large halves of eggshells for pots, and an old spoon for getting a bit of dirt out of a flowerbed. Fill shell halves nearly full of soil. Sprinkle the grass seed on top, and then add a thin layer of pulverized soil to cover the seed. Water carefully, to avoid a washout. This part of the operation can be well handled with the tiny pitcher from a set of doll dishes. Or water the eggshell garden with an eyedropper or a teaspoon.

On the third day the grass seeds will begin to sprout. By the fourth, the garden will be green—and by the time the grass plants are a week old, they will be an inch or two high.

Make a potato porcupine. Select a rather pointed Irish potato, and scoop out the middle leaving a shell thick enough to be sturdy. Press in thumbtacks for eyes, a bit of pipecleaner for a tail, and four twigs for legs. Fill the hollow with dirt, plant with millet (birdseed still does fine), and water regularly. In three or four days the porcupine will have a fine crop of bristles.

Plant a floating garden by sprinkling birdseed on cork coasters (or cork bottle-top liners or shapes cut from sheet cork). Float in a shallow bowl of water on a sunny windowsill. Landscape with pretty rocks.

Be sure you make it clear that this is *grass* seed. We call it birdseed because birds love to eat it, not because it will grow birds! Birds come from eggs, which is another part of God's plan.

This is a good time to talk about the orderly, dependable world God has created. If we plant grass seed, it grows grass. Grass seed *never* produces watermelons. What would happen if a watermelon grew in our eggshell garden? Or, if a farmer planted a whole field of corn to feed his family for the winter, and what came up was grass burrs? To marvel at God's plan for the universe is to experience worship.

Look at a flower. Take time to gaze at it, unhurriedly, as little children already know how to do. We tall ones are too often like Peter Bell, of whom Wordsworth said, "A primrose by the river's brim, a yellow primrose was to him—And it was nothing more."

Plant a water garden. Place a few sprigs of ivy or bright-leafed coleus or philodendron in clear glass vases of water. This is a good project for apartment dwellers, who may live several stories up and far removed from the soil. Keep water fresh and sweet, and use water garden fertilizers occasionally.

Plant citrus seeds. Orange, lemon, and grapefruit seed produce beautiful little dark green shiny-leafed plants. But plant several seeds, because they are sometimes reluctant to sprout.

Plant a vegetable garden. What better way to appreciate the bounty of God's plant world! Even a couple of tomato plants or a row of radishes in a flower bed can be a good summertime project. You may need to remind the child that if you "help" the plant too much, it will not grow. We who are parents need to remind ourselves occasionally that this is also true of children.

Go to a farm to pick vegetables. Watch ads in your local newspaper. Even big city papers often carry them, from mid-summer until fall: "Beans by the bushel. You pick." Or corn or okra or black-eyed peas—or squash and bell peppers and cucumbers—or fruit. When we let children grow up thinking that their food comes from a grocery store, we deprive them of

9

a feeling of real dependence upon the soil, and upon the work of other people—and upon the goodness of God. (Some present-day thinkers see the alienation of man from nature as the source of his alienation from other people, from himself, and from God.)

Let children participate, sometimes, in making jelly from scratch, beginning with fresh plums or berries or peaches or Concord grapes. Let them help bake bread or help put peaches away in the freezer. Undertake intentionally some projects that will reinforce this concept of our dependence upon the soil—upon God's plan for growing things—for the very food we eat.

Use as a table grace sometimes the old poem:

> Back of the bread is the snowy flour,
> And back of the flour the mill,
> And back of the mill is the wheat and the shower,
> And the sun and the Father's will. [2]

Plant an herb garden. Make room on a sunny windowsill for little pots of parsley, mint, marjoram, and chives. Plant your own seed, or purchase "punch-and-grow" kits.

Admire a crocus. Stoop down beside your child to see, close up, the courage of a crocus, or a daffodil, that will knife its way up through the still hard, still cold, perhaps still snow-covered ground, confident that spring really *is* going to happen.

Grow bean sprouts. Purchase a little package of mung beans from a food store or import shop. Place some (½ cup or so) in a quart jar, and cover with water overnight. (Punch holes in the jar lid. A four-year-old can do this alone, with a hammer and a

2. "A Grace," *The Book of Worship for Church and Home* (Nashville: The Methodist Publishing House, 1952), p. 364. Reprinted by permission.

good strong nail.) Next morning, drain the water off the beans, add fresh water, and promptly drain that off, too—draining through the holes in the lid. Place the jar of beans (wet, but not in water) in a dark place, such as a usually closed kitchen cupboard. Twice daily, cover with water and drain off again. The child will enjoy doing this. Beans will sprout in three days and be long enough to use in six. Use the bean sprouts in chow mein or in sauteed vegetables or add them to a salad—a reminder again that the foods we eat are grown naturally.

Gather dandelion greens. Be sure they are washed well, and use them in a salad.

Gather dandelion blossoms. Pick a bowlful of the yellow flowers, wash well, dip in batter, and fry. Delicious! Batter? Mix one egg, beaten with enough milk to make ½ cup liquid, with ½ cup flour, 1¼ teaspoons baking powder, one tablespoon melted butter or salad oil, salt, and pepper. (This batter also makes good french-fried squash blossoms, onion rings, sliced okra, cauliflower flowerettes, etc.)

Watch a bulb grow. Plant paper-white narcissus bulbs. Fill a small bowl four inches deep with clean washed pebbles. (It's fun to gather the pebbles from an old stream bed—or from a driveway. And it's fun to wash them, to watch them dance with bright new colors when they are wet.) Plant with at least three inches of pebbles below the bulbs. Keep water level just touching the bottoms of the bulbs. Place in a dark, cool spot until foilage is six or eight inches tall—then move to bright light. You and the child may wish to plant two bowls of bulbs—one to watch and one to share. How like a miracle that there should be such life and beauty hidden in that brown and ugly bulb!

Plant hyacinth bulbs. If you use a special hyacinth glass, you may watch the fascinating roots grow, as well as leaves, bud, and glorious blossoms. The lovely fragrance of hyacinth is like distilled essence of springtime.

Watch a potted amaryllis grow. The stalk shoots up rapidly, and the blooms are vivid trumpets. Again, quite amazing that *all that life and color* should lie dormant in a drab bulb. What God hath wrought!

Buy a flower. Dad may invite the child to go with him to buy a pot of red tulips for mom's valentine. Or the child may help select flowers or a plant for a neighbor who is ill.

Or, if you are driving home from a visit to the dentist and see a street-person selling flowers, *spend* a quarter for one beautiful carnation or a single fragrant rose. Sometimes we look at it more closely when there is just one. As one preschooler expressed it, "When you *look* at the world, you can't see it all at once. You have to look at it one at a time."

Do look at it, and use this moment, too, to become more aware of the beauties of creation.

It was Sadi, a sheik who lived seven hundred years ago, who said:

> If of thy moral goods
>   thou are bereft,
> And from thy slender store
>   two loaves alone to thee are left,
> Sell one, and with the dole
>   buy hyacinths to feed thy soul.

Make natural teas. Gather leaves of blackberry, raspberry, or strawberry plants—or mint or clover or goldenrod—on a sunny fall day. Tie them in bunches to dry. When they are dry and crumbly, crush them to make tea leaves. On cold, winter afternoons, brew a pot of tea from your own leaves. (One teaspoon of dried leaves per cup of boiling water, steeped for ten minutes or so. The tea will be pale, like many of the oriental teas.) Savor not only the tea but the fun you had last fall gathering the leaves. (Not all leaves are safe to eat, remember. Those listed *are* safe, and they make savory teas.)

Make a terrarium. Create a jungle, with overhanging foliage. The child's imagination can create all sorts of fancies (using bark, rocks, and tiny creatures), within the bounds of a three-pound peanut butter jar! No jar big enough? Ask someone at a nearby cafeteria to save you a one-gallon mayonnaise or pickle jar.

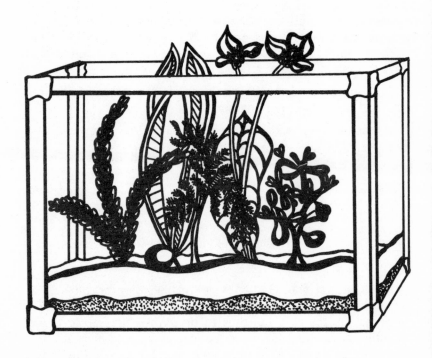

Root and plant a cutting. Ivies, geraniums, and begonias are the easiest to do. Cut just below a leaf joint, and put in a clear glass of water in the sun. When there are three or four good roots, plant carefully in soil. Potting soil is available in the dime-store, if some can't be borrowed from a flower bed. The container may be a clay pot, or a tin can with holes punched in it. (Set it in a saucer or a lid to prevent a water-stained windowsill.) What miracles of growth are these! Beautiful new plants—from a seed, from a bulb—from a potato, or even a *piece* of a potato —from a piece of carrot or beet—and now even from a *leaf.* This is, indeed, our Father's world, where all sorts of lovely things can happen!

Grow a carrot. Plant a carrot top in a pot of soil or in a saucer of pebbles and water, and soon you will have new leaves, pretty as any fern. A carrot can even be its own container, if you're willing to sacrifice half a large carrot to the project. Hollow out the core. Thread a light string or stout thread through the sides of the carrot to hang it by, and keep the hollow filled with water. Leaves will grow out the bottom, and then turn and begin climbing up the sides of the carrot!

A child is "spontaneity incarnate." The wise adult will learn to emulate the child's ability to seize the moment at hand. That is, one may not be able to plan to plant carrots next Tuesday at three. It is likely to be a more satisfying experience if it just happens. You and the child are putting up the groceries. The child pulls a sheaf of carrots out of the sack. Seeing them triggers your memory: "Say, let's plant a carrot top, and see what happens!"

3

Explore the Great Outdoors

Spend the night outside. On a camp out; or a picnic at the beach (even if you have to go back home again before midnight); or even in your own backyard. Have a campfire to sing around, and oh yes, let the lighting of the campfire be done ritually. Someone in the family may wish to read, or say, the words of John Oxenham's poem while the firelighters kneel with their matches to put flame to tinder and kindling, and then sit back on their haunches to watch the magic of the fire—in a moment of worship.

> Kneel always when you light a fire!
> Kneel reverently, and thankful be
> For God's unfailing charity,
> And on the ascending flame inspire
> A little prayer, that shall upbear
> The incense of your thankfulness
> For this sweet grace
> Of warmth and light!
> For here again is sacrifice
> For your delight. [3]

Then make this prayer, this ritual lighting of fire, a family tradition.

---

3. John Oxenham, "The Sacrament of Fire," *The Te Deums and the Sacraments* (Philadelphia: Pilgrim Press, 1928). Used by permission.

Sleep out—under stars. What nicer way to grow familiar with the night, to learn to feel comfortable with the dark.

"Isn't it nice that we have *dark* at night? It's so peaceful, so restful. Even the little birds are glad. They start early . . . when the sun is just thinking about going down. 'Oh, good,' they must say. 'It's going to be dark, so we can sleep and rest.' And they twitter quite a bit as they get all settled for the night." (Call your child some early evening to listen as the sparrows begin their "vespers." If the tiny little birds feel good about the approach of darkness, why need a child be afraid? This needs to be articulated, however, for many children *are* afraid of the dark and need repeated comfortable and comforting experiences in and with the dark.)

Sleep out, then. Lie in the grass on a mattress pad or bedroll and look up at the stars. The Bible expresses it best:

> The heavens are telling the glory of God;
>> and the firmament proclaims his handiwork.
>
> Day to day pours forth speech,
>> and night to night declares knowledge.
>
> There is no speech, nor are there words;
>> their voice is not heard;
>
> yet their voice goes out through all the earth,
>> and their words to the end of the world.
>>> (Psalm 19:1-4)

> When I look at thy heavens, the work of thy
> fingers,
> the moon and the stars which thou hast
> established;
> what is man that thou art mindful of him,
>> and the son of man that thou dost care for
>> him? . . .
> O Lord, our Lord,
>> how majestic is thy name in all the earth!
>>> (Psalm 8:3-4, 9)

Find the Big Dipper or Orion. The dipper is familiar to most

18

people. Orion can be located by the three stars in a row making his belt. Read or recall that the prophet Amos, in about 800 B. C., saw these same stars and said: "He who made the Pleiades and Orion, and turns deep darkness into the morning, and darkens the day into night, who calls for the waters of the sea, and pours them out (as rain) upon the surface of the earth, the Lord is his name" (Amos 5:8).

Wish on a star, and then make it a prayer:

> Star light, star bright,
> first star I see tonight,
> I wish I may, I wish I might
> have the wish I wish tonight. . . .
>
> Oh star, so far,
>   deep in the night,
>   this I desire:
> Let me, like thee,
>   be by His light,
>   a thing on fire.[4]

Grow sleepy in the good dark, under the mystical stars, and even as you fall asleep you have known a moment of worship.

Sing around the fire. Sing thanks to God for beauty and love.

And tell stories! There are so many *good* ones for campfire telling. There is real magic in Byrd Baylor Schweitzer's book *One Small Blue Bead.* It is one of those rare stories that children can understand, and grown-ups appreciate, and all remember and enjoy hearing again.

Some of the Bible stories are especially appropriate for telling in a campfire setting, including those stories of David the shepherd boy, of David and Jonathan, and of David playing his lyre for the distraught king. Read the gentle, powerful story of

---

4. Second stanza by Jo Carr.

creation from *God's Trombones*. And then, back home, for your own enrichment and delight, read the whole book.

A lovely story of helping others is the chapter called "The Bent Backs of Chang 'Dong" from *The Ugly American*. Your library probably has it. Check it out before you go, and read it, or tell it, to the family as they sit around the fire.

Don't forget the fun of *family* stories. Grandmother tells about the time when Daddy was about the size of Tad, here, when they went on a fishing trip, and he caught the biggest fish of all. Avoid laughing at, or "telling on" a child, even a long-ago child. But enjoy sharing the fun things and the adventures, the joys and sorrows and high moments of the family's past.

End your campfire time with a prayer of thanksgiving—or a prayer hymn:

> Breathe on me, Breath of God,
> Fill me with life anew,
> That I may love what Thou dost love,
> And do what Thou wouldst do.

> Edwin Hatch

or:

> Blessed be the tie that binds
> our hearts in Christian love.

> John Fawcett

There is something magic and memorable about a campfire—even if it is laid in an old wheel-less wheelbarrow of sand in the backyard—with neighbors invited over, perhaps, to share the toasting of marshmallows and the stories and the songs—and the prayer and the time of worship.

Make mudpies. Build sand castles.

Go to the park. Feed the ducks. Throw crumbs to the squirrels. Watch the fountain. *This* is God's world.

Take the time it takes for these things. It requires only a moment, after all, to admire a proffered dandelion. And when the child calls, "Oh, come see!" remember that there are times when the progress of an inchworm is of more profound significance than dishes undone or dust on the mantel. "Inchworm, inchworm, measuring the marigold. . . ." This—all this—is of God.

Bring the outdoors in. Bring in one brilliant maple leaf or a small branch of sumac. Enjoy the colors of autumn leaves, and talk about God's plan for seasons. Read Genesis 8:22:

> While the earth remains,
> seedtime and harvest,
> cold and heat,
> summer and winter,
> day and night,
> shall not cease.

But read it from the Bible. Let the child associate some of the words with that particular book. The Bible will not seem so formidable as the child grows up having seen it used and enjoyed.

In early spring bring in pussywillow branches. (My neighbor does what she refers to as "intentional pruning." All bushes need it, she maintains, but she gets to choose when it takes place. So she waits until she needs Christmas greenery to prune her juniper bush; and she waits until spring to prune the pussywillow—sharing both with others.) Bring in willow branches or white birch, which is soon covered with tiny, pale, bright leaves of spring, and even produces its own furry catkins. Bring in a spray of dogwood from the yard, or lilac, forsythia, crabapple, or quince. Watch them open indoors, as preview of what will be happening soon *outdoors.*

If a walk in the woods is a possibility for you and your child, go for such a walk. Take a small branch from this bush, or that—

most carefully, as one would *prune* rather than *molest* a bush—
and bring them home for a "surprise" arrangement. What fun to
watch bare branches come to life indoors. Buds swell, sprouts
develop—each branch a surprise, each a different and lovely
herald of spring. Read again, *from the Bible,* Genesis 8:22, and
rejoice in God's plan for seasons.

> Thank you, God,
>   for spring,
> When pussywillows happen.

Go barefooted. Get close to the earth. Help your child feel at
home with the earth. Remember aloud the words of a singing
commercial of a few years ago:

> Treat the earth kindly,
> Walk on it gently,
> Speak to it sweetly,
> Cherish its name. [5]

It is God who created the earth and who entrusted it to us.

5. Used by permission.

Touch a touch-me-not (technically "balsam"). The fat little seed pods will "rip at the seams," sending the seeds flying out, at just a touch. Such fun! Sometimes grandmothers plant these in the flower bed just because of the fun they provide for children.

Lord Baden-Powell, founder of Boy Scouts, referred to it as "this jolly world"! Ah, yes! And learning to feel at home in the world is part of a growing faith.

Let the children make the most of their wonder years. Let them hear with their ears the song of a cricket and see with awe the masterpiece through the windowpane.

Look at a larkspur. See how like a rabbit's head the blossom looks—a rabbit who wears a bright collar of petals.

Show your child how to squeeze—so gently—the "jaws" of a snapdragon blossom, to make the dragon snap.

Touch a sensitive plant, and see the leaves fold up, protectively.

Pop the seed pods on a lupine.

Keep a cocoon, and watch the wonder of an emerging butterfly.

Marvel at an insect. There seems to be some sort of natural affinity between a child and a bug. No wonder! Here is an amazing little creature, far smaller and weaker than the child, who can do prodigious feats! Hop—as high as the "giant" child's own head. Fly—drifting gracefully over a flower bed or darting like a dragonfly from one unmarkable spot in the air to another. An ant can carry a load several times its size and can work in colonies for the common good of all. Insects make honey; build adobe houses; dig tunnels, or funnels; lay eggs, raise families, and go stalking through the jungle of grass in search of prey. No wonder the child is entranced.

Enjoy this wonder with your child. Watch the marvel of a cicada, breaking out of the imprisoning crusty shell of its old earthy life, its wings like limp bits of old lettuce until they begin to stretch and grow and dry, and become (ah, miracle!) the delicate sturdy vehicles to make it airborne! All this, mind you, in twenty minutes, and before your very eyes!

This might be a good time to remember with your child the delightful hymn that says it so well:

> All things bright and beautiful,
> All creatures great and small,
> All things wise and wonderful:
> The Lord God made them all.
>
> Each little flower that opens,
> Each little bird that sings,
> He made their glowing colors,
> He made their tiny wings.

Cecil Frances Alexander

Notice wings—the lacy wings of mayfly or dragonfly, bright butterfly wings—the soft velvet of moth wings—and ladybugs, with sturdy wing-covers carefully "enameled."

Buy a jar of honey with a piece of honeycomb in it. Talk about the many marvels of bees. Don't overload your child with pedantic lectures, but do appreciate not only the honey but the tiny workers who made it.

Life can be full of miracles, and for the very young or the very perceptive a miracle can be a stone with a special color or a mushroom, whole and perfect.

Harvest a weed. Take a can of hairspray or any color spray paint to the meadow or vacant lot where milkweed has produced its oversized puffballs. Spray a few to set the seeds so they won't

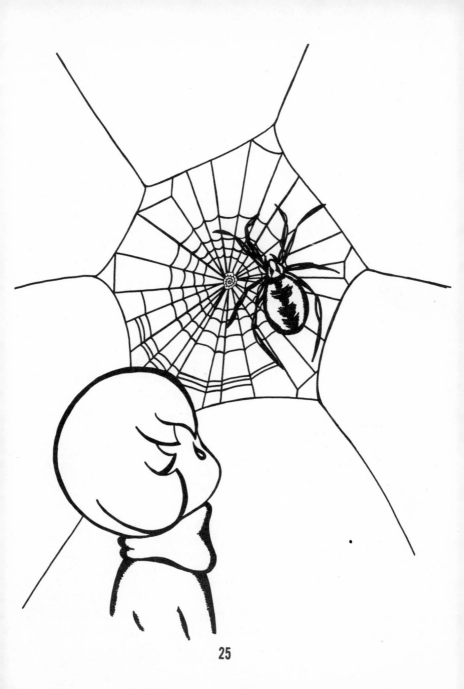

blow away. Then pick them carefully and take them home for an interest center—nay, for a *worship* center! How exquisite the design! How beautiful indeed is our Father's world.

Make a spore print. Some magic morning your child may find toadstools on the lawn. (Remember, some varieties are poisonous.) Pick two. Carefully twist out the stems, and place one mushroom or toadstool cap on a piece of dark colored construction paper, one on a piece of white paper. Cover each with a glass to protect it from stray breezes or other movement, and leave it quite alone for twenty-four hours. When you lift the glass, you find a star-burst! The radiating gills have shed their spores, in delicate lines, to create a beautiful picture.

Look at the mushroom. Look at the spore print. Talk about the *little* beauties in God's world—or about the glory of creation —or about how much fun God must have had creating mushrooms!

The child may want to mount the best spore print on the wall or on the kitchen bulletin board, to remind everyone of the wonder.

Blow a dandelion. Watch the tiny parachutes carry their seed-loads to plant themselves in other parts of the lawn. Talk about ways other seeds get scattered. Maple seeds whirl to the ground like tiny helicopters. (Gather some maple seeds, if ever you have the opportunity, and play with them, throwing them in the air to watch their gay descent. Save some to play with another day.) Elm seeds are like little ruffled frisbies that sail through the air. Grass burrs hitch rides on Janie's sock or on Rover's furry foot. When we say, "Apple core, Baltimore" and then throw away the core, we may be planting an apple tree! How remarkable is God's plan!

And how *bountiful!* Look how *many* tiny parachutes-with-seeds come from a single ball of dandelion. Consider, and help

your child consider, the generosity of a creator whose plan is that one apple seed can grow into a tree producing bushels of apples every year, and each one of those apples has several seeds in it, each of which is capable of producing, ad infinitum. Praise God, from whom all such blessings flow!

Make a bird feeder. Explore a stream.

Go adventuring with a magnifying glass. Look at the veins in a leaf. Look at a June bug—face to face. It looks like a friendly puppy, only with those two ridiculous palm-like antennae waving over its face. Look at a daddy longlegs, with its eyes on long towers in the middle of its back. Look at an aphid, an ant, a flower, a piece of bark.

Look at a leaf of grass. Marvel at it. "A mouse," said Walt Whitman, "is miracle enough to stagger sextillions of infidels."[6] And really to *see* what we usually merely look at makes fireworks happen inside us.

Remember that a small child's interest span is short. To force any "adventure" beyond the child's own interest in it would be to undo more than you've done. Just relax, and enjoy it together. Then go in and make lemonade, and enjoy that, too.

Enjoy the weather. Talk about these *good* hot July days— good growing weather for corn. They say that corn grows so fast on a hot summer day that one can hear it creak and groan as it stretches upward. It is good growing weather for children and their privileged grown-up companions, too. Walk together in the grass, barefooted, and enjoy the cool of it, the soft green of it. Chase a butterfly in the city park—not so much to catch it as to rejoice with it in the freedom of a summer's day. Go on a picnic. Play in the sprinkler. Climb a tree. Read a book, to-

---

6. Walt Whitman, "Song of Myself," *Leaves of Grass* (New York: Doubleday Doran and Co., 1940), p. 68.

gether, under the tree, in the shade. Thank God for shade and sun and ladybugs. Thank God for summer days.

And when you get back home again, find the place in the Bible (Psalm 118:24) where it says: *"This* is the day which the Lord has made; let us rejoice and be glad in it."

Look at a spider web. Marvel at its design and symmetry. Someday you may chance upon a spider just beginning to spin her web. Take time to appreciate what she is doing. See how she takes advantage of a bit of breeze to anchor her web to a bush or to a twig or to the edge of the house. Notice, with your child, her persistence and patience and her dedication to the design.

Celebrate Indian summer. Look for pretty autumn leaves. Put some in a pottery jug. Pin a few on the bulletin board. Rake leaves. Dance in leaves. Listen to dry leaves crunch under foot when you go for a walk.

Preserve some small and still-soft leaves by placing them on a cut circle of colored paper and covering them with a circle of clear, adhesive paper. (Con-tak is one brand. This is a very simple craft that even a three-year-old can do and feel so pleased with the results.)

Celebrate autumn. Buy a pumpkin and cut a jack-o-lantern. Afterwards, peel and boil and mash the pumpkin and make it into a pumpkin pie. Reinforce by this act the mostly hearsay concept for the city child that our food really *does* come from the earth.

Thank God for pumpkins, and autumn, and the roundness of the seasons.

Enjoy a storm. Share in the excitement of the pre-storm winds. Watch trees bend gracefully before them. Smell the

approaching rain. Stand out on the porch, on the walk, on the balcony, in the yard—where you can see the sky and feel the wind, and take deep, exhilarating gulps of rain-sweet air.

Play in the rain. When a summer rain begins with those monstrous drops that make big round dollops on the sidewalk, skip and play among the drops, rejoicing in God's gift of rain to the thirsty earth.

Or go for a walk in the rain—barefooted, bareheaded, if it's that sort of rain, or in slickers and rubber boots. Slosh and splash.

Or take time to make a boat with your child. Point a 1 x 4 (or a piece of apple-box end). Add a block of wood for a deck. Put nails around the edge. Add string for a rail, and a good strong string to pull it by.

Sing "Singing in the Rain."

Celebrate rain! *Enjoy* it. And, in joy, praise God for it. This is no moralistic, lecture-all-the-time lifestyle. Rather it is an at-home-in-the-world-ness.

Celebrate snow. Bundle up and go for a walk and see what beauty the snow has created on a chainlink fence—in a vacant lot full of weeds—in a green hedge or a clump of trees. How graceful everything looks—even the little red wagon that got left outside. How pure the world seems!

Make a snowman, with a carrot for a nose—lumps of coal or rocks for eyes—and a curved twig for a grin. Borrow a hat for him. Make a snow lady, a snow boy and girl, a snow bunny, a pup.

Slide down a gentle hill on an inflated inner tube, together.

Make snow angels. Lie down on your back in a patch of clean, untrampled snow, arms and legs outstretched. Bring legs together, scraping away the snow between them, to create the angel's skirt. Make wings with wide, sweeping motions of the arms. Then get up and walk carefully away and look back at your snow image, to see what you have done!

Come back inside to enjoy a warm house, dry clothes, and a cup of hot cocoa, and to pause for a prayer of thanksgiving. We *celebrate* winter, and thank God for his good plan.

Make snow ice cream. Beat well two eggs and some milk, with a pinch of salt, a good dollop of powdered sugar and a spoonful of vanilla. *When this is ready,* run out and get a big pan full of clean snow. Stir fast, and eat it right then—scarcely anything tastes so good.

4

Observe the Holidays Together

Enjoy Easter! Joy—that's what Easter is all about! It is the church's testimony to the great good news, brought to despairing disciples, that the Christ who had taught them how to live, and then who had himself been put to death was alive, was risen! This testimony was joy indeed.

Was? Is! Because joy and new life are what Easter is all about.

The events of Holy Week, though, are not easy to explain to a child. Christmas is a different matter. A little new baby and the warmth of a borrowed stable are things children can understand. But the Easter story is one of cruelty and death. A grown man—son of God—is brutally executed on a cross. We subconsciously rate it *R* and gloss it over at home. We feel a little guilty about an alternative emphasis on Easter baskets and new clothes. We mumble something about "they'll understand, of course, when they are older," and even as we mumble, wonder sometimes how well we ourselves understand. This year, though, let's capture for our children and ourselves some of the joy that Easter really means.

You may wish to read aloud the account of the first Easter from Mary Alice Jones's *Tell Me About Jesus*. And then look for daily, understandable ways in which to underline the meaning of what was read.

The customs of the season which we commonly call secular did not just happen. Many of them are the outgrowth of people's search for the expression of truth. A few words of explanation to the child about the meaning of the custom can add a feeling of worship which we have so often missed.

Coloring eggs, for instance, can be done in observance of the real meaning of Easter. Eggs *are* a symbol of new life, if we stop to think of it so. Life, wrapped in a confining shell—until . . . behold! A chick pecks open the shell, and a real and vivid new creature steps forth. So dye the eggs (traditionally yellow, for the returning sun of springtime, purple for the King of life, and red for joy) in the good, warm-smelling, hint-of-vinegar kitchen. And speak of them as symbols of new life, as you work. Speak of the significance of the colors. Tell about the custom in old Bulgaria of placing the first dyed egg in front of the kitchen icon, the worship-center picture of Christ, with a candle beside it, as a symbol of the resurrection. Maybe the child will say, "Let's do that, too!" And lo, a moment of worship, right in the middle of dying the eggs.

Or serve pretzels, in observance of Easter, as has long been the custom in parts of Europe. *Pretzel* is a German contraction for the Latin word meaning *arms*. Pretzels were first baked for Lent, to take the place of bread. Milk and eggs and fats were forbidden during Lent, and these little loops of bread are made only of flour and water and salt. And they are twisted to form two arms crossed in the act of prayer. Serving pretzels can be only a gimmick, or it can be a genuine reminder of the historic church and a call to reverence.

Hot cross buns, served *thoughtfully* on Good Friday or on

Easter morning, can become not only a family tradition but the basis of a meal of remembrance and communion.

If the children have new clothes for Easter, then let them be in deliberate observance of the holy day. The mother making new clothes for her children can speak of the joyful custom observed by the early Christians of wearing new clothes for Easter, casting off that which was old, and putting on clean new raiment, that we may step forward in newness of life. And as the family leaves for church on Easter morning, say it again.

There is another, simple, no-words-needed way to say what Easter means. Stop by the church sanctuary on Friday evening, just for a quiet family moment. The church will seem empty, dark. And then, on Easter Sunday morning—behold, the same sanctuary, now full of sunlight and flowers and jubilant music!

Take a walk together, looking for signs of spring. Drive to the park and picnic there. Or just walk around the block or the yard. Then take the same walk a week or two later. Talk about the changes that have taken place.

Bring the outdoors in. Watch buds on a branch of crabapple or plum unfold. Watch what happens to pussywillow. Keep a rebus list of springtime discoveries on the kitchen bulletin board. Look for the first robin or crocus or the first greening of the willow tree.

Plant a bulb, in observance of Easter. Linger around the supper table on a cold winter evening to plant a hyacinth bulb, and speak of its blooming in time for Easter. Plant another, perhaps, for an elderly neighbor to enjoy. When the bulbs *do* bloom, they are beautiful and fragrant reminders of new life, emerged from a dry, "dead" bulb.

Watch spring happen as crocuses knife through the snow to proclaim new life, and as "dead" willow switches begin to green.

You may wish to make it vocal in the words of Aileen Fisher's poem:

> Now everything is bright again,
> all up and down the world.
> The tendrils that were tight, again
> are magically uncurled.
>
> And voices start to sing again,
> and eyes begin to see
> the worth of everything again,
> as Easter turns the key.
>
> And mankind feels the pull again
> of Something from above,
> And everyone is full again
> of faith, and hope, and love . . .
> And everyone is full again
> of faith, and hope, and love. [7]

Give thanks at Thanksgiving. Give thanks traditionally, holding hands with family and friends around the table. The table may be spread with simple fare or laden with turkey and dressing, cranberry relish, and mince pie. Or, it may be a sacrificial meal.

But let not the simplicity of the meal, the magnificence of the feast, or the significance of the sacrifice blind us to the thanks we owe to God, whose benevolence and whose sacrifice we but dimly comprehend.

A child enjoys hearing the story of the first Thanksgiving—of how even in hardship the Pilgrim fathers remembered that God was with them and that there were blessings for which to be grateful.

---

7. From "Eastern Morn," by Aileen Fisher. Reprinted by permission from *Holiday Programs for Boys and Girls* by Aileen Fisher. Plays, Inc., Publishers, Boston, MA02116. Copyright © 1953 by Aileen Fisher.

A child may enjoy hearing a poem-prayer of Pilgrim children:

> On the first Thanksgiving, long long ago
> Three little children stood in a row
> By the loaded table of rough new wood
> And thanked the Lord for all things good.
> Jonathan whispered a little prayer
> Thanking God for the crisp fall air,
> For turkey and deer to give them meat,
> For ears of corn so good and sweet.
> For a log house home in a strange new land,
> For a brave and humble pilgrim band.
> Little Patience started to say
> "Thank you, God, for a happy day."
> And then she added, "Thank You, too,
> For my corn husk doll in calico blue,
> For my friend Small Dove, with the black, black hair,
> And for your wise and loving care."
> Peace said, "Thank you, God, today,
> For our Indian friends, and the helpful way
> They have taught us how to plant and grow
> These strange new foods that we didn't know!
> Pumpkins I'd never seen—but my!
> They do make the tastiest pumpkin pie!"
> On the first Thanksgiving, long, long ago,
> Three little children stood in a row
> By the loaded table of rough new wood
> And thanked the Lord for all things good. [8]

The child may enjoy drawing pictures of that first Thanksgiving, as well as helping with the preparations for this year's enactment of it.

Remember to express gratitude for simple turkey sandwiches on the day after. If we should express thanks each day for every gift received, our lives would be "thanksliving."

---

8. Jo Carr in *Primary Teaching Pictures* (Nashville: The Methodist Publishing House, November, 1962). Reprinted by permission.

The season of Advent. One *cycle* of home worship experiences can be built around the family observance of Advent. Some churches make available printed suggestions for home worship, including the lighting of the Advent candles on the four Sundays before Christmas, with an additional ceremony for Christmas day. Adapt such suggestions to the ages of the children in your own family. Or use some of the ideas on the following pages. Or (better still) compose your own Advent ceremonies.

Make an Advent wreath. Simply arrange Christmas greenery in a circle, on the mantel, or on a little table, or wherever it seems to belong, and place around it four candles, traditionally purple, the color of royalty, for the four Sundays of Advent, with a white Christ candle in the center of the circle.

Or purchase an inexpensive styrofoam ring, and cut four candle holes in it and arrange bits of ground pine or English ivy or holly (or the trimmings from the juniper bush that you have waited till now to prune) around it. Place the white candle, in a simple holder, in the center of the wreath. The preschooler will love helping with all this.

Choose a place to put the Advent wreath. Make it a family worship center, if you wish to think of it as such. The child may wish to arrange the crèche beside it.

Observe Advent. Choose a time, each of the four Sundays of Advent, when the family can observe together the lighting of the Advent candle. Here are suggested ways of saying what the Advent wreath is all about:

First Sunday of Advent: "Let Every Heart Prepare Him Room"

> *Father:* Today is a special day, for it is the beginning of our celebration of Christmas. *Advent* is a word that means *to come.* It is a time of get-

ting ready, of preparing ourselves for the *coming* of Christ.

Mother: That is what we are doing now, preparing ourselves for Christmas. An Advent wreath is an old custom, but like carols and the crèche, it seems new, brand new, every year. Its circle reminds us of God, without beginning

or end. Its candles are for the light that came into the world with the *advent,* with the coming of the Christ child.

Older Child: *(Reading Isaiah 9:2, 6a)*

The people who walked in darkness
    have seen a great light;
those who dwelt in a land of deep darkness,
    on them has light shined.
For to us a child is born!

Father: __(Name of child)__ will light the first candle. *(Helps small child light candle)* It reminds us that we should get our hearts ready, as well as our homes, for Christmas.

All: *(Sing first verse of "Joy to the World")*

Mother: Let every heart prepare him room. Let each one of us prepare a place in our celebration of Christmas for Christ himself. This is what the giving, the remembering, the cards, the lists, the gifts, and the baking are all about.

Prayer: Dear God, help us prepare our hearts for the coming of Jesus.

Second Sunday of Advent: "Love Came Down at Christmas"

Father: This is the second Sunday of the Advent season. We come together in a time of quiet, in which we can get ourselves ready for the coming of Christmas.

Mother: *(Helps small child relight first candle)* Last Sunday we lighted the first Advent candle to remind us that this is a time of getting ready.

Older Child: Today we light the second Advent candle to tell us that the meaning of Christmas is love. *(Lights second candle)*

41

All: *(To be sung or read aloud as a worship poem)*

> Love came down at Christmas,
> Love all lovely, Love Divine;
> Love was born at Christmas;
> Stars and angels gave the sign.

Christina G. Rossetti

Mother: Jesus came to tell us of God's love for us and to teach us how to love God and each other.

Father: *(Read Luke 2:1-7)*

All: *(Sing a familiar carol such as "Away in a Manger.")*

Prayer: Dear God, we thank you for the love that Christmas is all about. Amen.

Third Sunday of Advent: "Joy to the World"

Father: This is the third Sunday of the Advent season. *(Helps small child relight first candle)* On the first Sunday of Advent, we lighted a candle to remind us to get ready in our hearts for the coming of Jesus.

Older Child: On the second Sunday of Advent, we lighted a candle to tell us that the meaning of Christmas is love. *(Lights second candle)*

Mother: *(Helps child light third candle)* Our third candle reminds us of the joy that Jesus' coming brought.

Father: Joy! That's what Christmas is all about. "There's a tumult of joy o'er the wonderful birth." The angel tried to explain it, "Behold, I bring you good news of a great *joy* ... " something to be radiant about—"for to you is born this day in the city of David a Savior, who is Christ the Lord" (Luke 2:10-11).

42

Mother:	Some folks got the message. The shepherds went back home glorifying and praising God for what they had seen. But lots of folks in Bethlehem did not understand. They went right on about their taxpaying and baking bread and weaving cloth as though Christmas had never happened at all.
Older Child:	When Jesus became a man, he tried again to explain "that my joy may be in you, and that your joy may be full" (John 15:11).
Father:	We can't *buy* joy. But joy happens when we get so caught up in what really took place in the stable at Bethlehem, that we, too, worship.
All:	*(Sing "Joy to the World")*
Prayer:	Dear God, we give thanks. For joy around us, joy within us, we give thanks. Amen.

Fourth Sunday of Advent: "What Can I Give Him?"

Father:	This is the fourth Sunday of the Advent season. Like the shepherds of Bethlehem and the Wise Men from the East, we, too, come to the manger to worship.
Mother:	*(Helps child light first candle)* The first candle reminds us to get ourselves ready for Christmas.
Older Child:	The second Advent candle tells us that Jesus came to teach us to love God and each other. *(Lights candle)*
Father:	*(Helps child light third candle)* The third candle reminds us of the joy that Jesus' coming brought.
Mother:	Today we light a candle for helping others. The love we have for God makes us want to

help others. This is the *giving* part of Christmas.

Father: *(Reads Matthew 2:1-12)* They came bringing gifts. But this is not the first Christmas, and Jesus is no longer a baby in a manger.

Child: So, then, how shall *we* come bringing gifts?

Older Child: We made a Christmas list. We have baked presents for some, bought presents for some, hammered and stitched presents for some. Does that count?

Mother: Yes, if we have done it with love. But there is another way, too.

All: *(Sing together, or read aloud)*

What can I give him,
Poor as I am?
If I were a shepherd,
I would bring a lamb;
If I were a wise man,
I would do my part;
Yet what I can I give him:
Give my heart.

Christina G. Rossetti

(This is the last verse of a carol, "In the Bleak Midwinter," which is included in many hymnals.)

Father: The only gift we can bring to the manger is love—love for all people, in memory of the love of God who gave his Son.

Prayer: Dear God, who gave us Christmas, let us be thinking now and all the rest of our lives of how we can give. Let our love for you be so great that it bubbles over into a love for all your children. Amen.

44

Christmas Day:

> *Father:* The season of Advent has brought us to this day of the coming of the Christ Child.

> *Older Child:* On the first Sunday of Advent, we lighted a candle to remind us of our need to get ready.

> *Mother:* *(Helps little child light second candle)* On the second Sunday we lighted the candle of love.

> *Father:* The third Sunday was for joy. *(Lights candle)*

> *Child:* Last Sunday we lighted a candle for giving. *(Lights fourth candle)*

> *Mother:* And now we have come to Christmas Day. We shall light the Christ candle, which stands for Jesus, the light of the world. *(Helps child light center candle)*

> *All:* *(Sing together)*

> > Infant holy, Infant lowly,
> > For His bed a cattle stall;
> > Oxen lowing, Little knowing
> > Christ the Babe is Lord of all.
> > Swift are winging Angels singing,
> > Noels ringing, Tidings bringing:
> > Christ the Babe is Lord of all.
> >
> > From the Polish
> > English words by E. M. G. Reed

> *Father:* *(Read John 1:1-5)*

> *Prayer:* Dear God, our heavenly Father, help us grow to be more loving. We know this is why Christmas happened. Amen.

So the lighting of candles and the ritual restatement of what Christmas is all about helps keep the TV commercials and the streetcorner Santas in perspective.

Jane Merchant put it rather well in her poem "Prayer for a Child:"

> Lord, I would not deny him
> Any gaieties
> Of Santa Claus and reindeer
> And wonder-laden trees.
> But let a song ring clearly
> And let a star shine through—
> And when he thinks of Christmas, Lord,
> Let him think of You. [9]

Keep Christmas. There are so *many* ways of making it the wonderful, joyous, Christ-centered season that it was meant to be!

Sing carols as you and your child make cookies or wash dishes or ride in the car. The carols keep us remembering what Christmas is all about.

Put carols on the record player, and let their music be background to all of December. (Firestone, Goodyear, Montgomery Ward, and several other companies issue beautiful collections of Christmas music annually, $1 for each long-playing record.)

Watch television. Enjoy together some of the TV specials (preselected). Dr. Seuss's *How the Grinch Stole Christmas,* for instance, is a delightful children's story and underscores in its own understandable way some of the deeper meanings of the season.

Make presents. The most *fun* kind of present to give is one you have made yourself. It is also, often, one of the nicest to receive.

---

9. *Together,* December 1956.   Reprinted by permission.

Bake cookies together, pretty Christmas cookies trimmed with bright icing and bits of candy. (And leave enough dough for "hand" cookies. Roll the dough out smoothly and have the child place his or her hand on it, fingers outstretched, while you cut carefully around it. Bake, sprinkle with sugar, and eat—hot from the oven! Getting ready for Christmas is such *fun!*)

Make candy. An easy recipe for the child to make is this one. The process is simple, the cooking minimal, and the results generous and delicious.

Instant Candy

Combine: 2 cups sugar
            ½ cup milk
            2 sticks oleo

Boil two minutes.

Remove from heat and add: 1 6-oz. package chocolate chips
                             ½ cup nuts
                             ½ cup coconut
                             3 cups oats
                             1 teaspoon vanilla
                             1/8 teaspoon salt

Drop by teaspoonfuls on waxed paper and allow to harden.

Equally easy to make, and *quite* attractive:

Holly Clusters

Melt: 30 regular-size marshmallows
        (this becomes a counting game)
        1 stick of oleo
Remove from heat and add: 3 cups cornflakes
                             1 teaspoon green food coloring
Drop by spoonfuls on waxed paper.
Add 3 redhots in a cluster on the one side of each "cookie."
The jagged edges of the cornflakes look remarkably like holly leaves, and the redhots like berries. The green-and-red color makes this a

decorative addition to any spread of Christmas goodies. And the child, of course, has obvious reason to be pleased with all the effort.

Make a cloved apple. Provide the child with a small firm apple and a box of whole cloves. Show how to punch the cloves into the apple, close enough together that they touch, but not so close that some stand out on top of others. Place the finished apple in the center of a square of gold net, and gather up and tie with gold or brown ribbon. The cloved apple makes a sweet-smelling gift that will last, literally, for years. And it is a project that even a four-year-old can do all alone.

Make a mini-bulletin board. Obtain a square or rectangular scrap of cellotex or ceiling tile. Cut a piece of solid-color cloth (a scrap of percale or broadcloth left over from a sewing project will do nicely) about two inches larger all around than the cellotex board. Put white glue all round the edges of the cloth, and glue it around the board, stretching the edges smooth. (The child will need help in getting the cloth on the board securely but can carry out the remainder of the project alone.) "Draw," with a thin line of glue, a flower stem, and place a piece of yarn on the line of glue, patting it down gently. "Draw" leaves with glue, and press down loops of yarn on the still-wet glue lines. Add a colorful blossom. The child will have fun creating different designs. Place an inexpensive note pad in the corner of the board, thumbtacking it through the tablet back. Add a short pencil on a piece of yarn, for a useful and attractive gift that will please both giver and receiver.

Making a gift can become a visible expression of love and can thus strengthen a valid concept of the meaning of Christmas.

Giving becomes even more significant with the added fun of the search for a totally *unexpecting* receiver. In such a case, let the gift be small so that it carries no burden of reciprocation. But making a gingerbread boy for "the nice lady who always checks us out at the grocery store" can be delightful fun—and it can be a way of recognizing the many ways in which *other* people enrich *our* lives.

So—*enjoy* the Christmas season. Take advantage of the many opportunities for doing fun things together. Let the child *help* make cookies, wrap packages, arrange the Christmas cards (and look at them and rearrange them and look some more) and make ropes of cranberries and popcorn for the tree. A big needle, doubled thread, a pan of popped corn, and a sack of cranberries may keep your child busy, off and on, for two or three days, as the lovely rope (three popcorns and then a cranberry, three popcorns and then a cranberry—chanted, sung, hummed, and greatly admired) grows longer and longer.

Let the child play with the manger scene and arrange the shepherds and the central figures. If the one you have is an heirloom, get another, expendable, one. Some families keep the Wise Men figures out of the scene until Christmas Eve, when the star appeared, and then place them clear across the room from the figures at the stable, moving them closer each day—to the windowsill, to the table, to the bookshelf, to the mantel—until finally, on the Twelfth Night (January 6) they reach the manger and worship the newborn king.

Enjoy the making and the giving of gifts, the singing of carols. Enjoy the good smells and the happy sounds of Christmas. And seize the opportunity, occasionally, to thank God for friends, for hot cocoa, for fun times together, and for the amazing love that became incarnate on that first Christmas and dwelt among us.

5

Grow Together

Have fun together! Blow bubbles and watch the many-splendored panes of color they reflect. Watch wild geese fly overhead and marvel at the wisdom that guides their flight. Have a race eating the scallops off a gingersnap. Let there be levity within the home that makes laughter possible, spontaneous, and often.

"Miss Frances" Horwich has written an intriguing and helpful book called *The Magic of Bringing Up Your Child.* She includes in it a few apropos comments on this matter of having *fun* together:

> Just imagine how it is for the child whose mother and father are both cheerless. His home is unpleasant, he is uneasy in it, and the outside world is to be feared. For such a child, life is just a thing that has to be endured . . . It comes down to this—
>
> *One:* When parents let gloom, anxiety, or any other variety of joylessness become a basic attitude, and thus an atmosphere that pervades the home and all its activities, they miss a great deal of life. Even so, it is their child who suffers most, because this is the atmosphere he has to grow up in, and because it will affect him, in one way or another, the rest of his days.

Two: Family fun is the result of an attitude that creates a pleasant home atmosphere. In such a warm, sunny "climate," laughter and good feeling well up naturally and often.

Three: Before a child can have fun with other children, he must experience fun with his parents. [10]

So have fun. Enjoy your child. Enjoy your life together. And thank God for the child and the life and the joy.

Watch children grow. Enable the child to watch *himself* or *herself* grow. Sit down together occasionally to look at your child's baby book. Talk about the pictures. Seeing snapshots of oneself as a tiny baby, as a cherub in a highchair, as a wobbly toddler will strengthen a child's awareness of how *big* he or she is getting to be.

Mark your child's growth. If your family lifestyle is such that you move often, make a growth chart that you can take with you—a long strip of sturdy paper or close-woven cloth (a strip of window-shade cloth makes a dandy one) which can be mounted on the wall and which records how tall the child was at one and a half, and then at two, and now at two and a half or three. (Do not get in the habit of marking your child's height more often than every six months. It can be demoralizing, at five, to discover that you haven't grown a smidge in a whole month!) Do mark the chart, ceremonially, on birthdays, and perhaps on half-birthdays as well.

Or mark the child's growth in the time-honored way, on a wall—on a closet door facing, writing in the date beside the name. (One mother of a son now grown called the painters in to show them the one closet facing board that was *not* to be repainted with the rest of the bedroom, for it held the measurements of a family growing up.) Wherever you make the marks,

10. Frances R. Horwich, *The Magic of Bringing Up Your Child* (New York: McGraw-Hill, 1959), pp. 118-120.

the child can see that they are *really* higher than last year's. Take the moment to thank God for the way the child is growing physically, and every other way.

A child wants to grow, desperately—to be taller, stronger, older, more important. This is true even when acting most like a baby. The child finds comfort and reassurance in knowing that growth really *is* taking place, and that growth will continue. This will make the child's "life among the giants" so much more tolerable.

In *two-by-fours,* his delightful booklet about little children, cartoonist Charles Schulz comments:

> Reassurance plays a considerable role during these years. . . . Reassurance for the child is finding Mother in the kitchen when he comes toddling out of the bedroom in the morning. It is having the same old beat-up toys lying around him in his room. It is going through the same routine at night—a bath, brushing his teeth, hearing a story, being tucked in bed with a prayer. It is being around adults who themselves are serene, not torn up by the tensions of an insecure world. [11]

Knowing that they are growing is reassuring to children. So is knowing that they are loved. Tell them so. Show them so. Undergird them with sure reminders of your unwavering love. Their concept of God's love will be in terms of the parental love experienced since the moment of birth.

So let your love for the child be supportive and enriching, and show that it is constant.

Play the game of stars. You might begin, one day, with an apple, talking about the old Bohemian custom of cutting an apple open on Christmas Day. If there is a star inside, then the year ahead will be a good one. Cut an apple then, and look at

---

11. Charles Schulz, *two-by-fours* (New York: Warner Press, 1965), pp. 9-10.

the star. The secret, of course, is to cut the apple crosswise, exposing the star. Ah! A star inside! A reminder, perhaps, of the star of Bethlehem, which pointed the way to the place where the young Child lay.

Look for such surprise stars in other places, all through the year. Look in seed patterns and blossom ends—in pears and oranges and pine cones—in roses and celery and squash. There is a tiny, darker, perfect little star in the knobby "knuckle" on the twig of a cottonwood tree. There is a lovely star engraved on a sand dollar. The starfish is a caricature of a star. And there is a star within a star within a star folded in the heart of a lowly cabbage. *"Mirabile dictu!* Come, see! I've found another star!" And it becomes a moment of worship, a time for thanking God for these secret, hidden reminders of the wonders of creation.

Squash a can! Cut both ends out of the corn can which was opened for lunch (and the tuna can for supper, and all the cans you open from now on). Peel off the paper label. Let the child do it. Then let the child step on the can to smash it flat and drop it into a sack to save for recycling. Explain that we do this to take care of the good earth which God created. We do this to save tin, so that it can be used again. We can thank God for this earth by saying a prayer of thanks. Another way to thank God is to squash a can. Need one separate the sacred and the secular? Both ways of saying thanks are valid, for all of life can glorify God.

Talk about people. Call to the attention of the little child the kind and helpful people in the world. "Daddy did that because he loves you." "See the policeman directing traffic? The policeman helps us." "I love you." "See the card grandmother sent? Grandmother loves you." Only after such experiences as this can the words *God loves you* have much meaning.

Hang a poster. Choose a bright, call-to-worship sort of poster. Get a poster catalog or visit a gift shop, and order one that you will enjoy living with for a while. There is one, for example, that is an excerpt from an e. e. cummings poem:

i thank You God for most this amazing day. [12]

Or make a poster, you and your child. Crayon or watercolor it. Or use felt-tip markers. Use squares and triangles and trumpets cut from gift-wrapping paper to make it jubilant. Find a verse in the Bible to write on it. Enjoy *making* it. Enjoy *hanging* it. And then just enjoy seeing it there on the wall.

Plant a seed. Say a prayer. Sing a song, in jubilance. It is in the quicksilver lovely moments of every day that we can best praise God, vocally, *in* that moment, before it gets away.

Read a book.

Tell stories. The little child who says "Daddy, tell me a story" is not a critic of plot, or of the nuances of character development. The child just wants to hear a simple story. Preferably about herself or himself. Preferably about some pleasant experience that really happened. "Once upon a time there was a little girl whose name was _____, and she had brown hair and dancing eyes, and her favorite dessert was strawberry ice cream. One day she and her daddy went downtown. They went into a big store, and they rode on the escalator. When they got to the third floor, they went over to the coffee shop. Daddy ordered a cup of coffee, but _____ ordered *strawberry* ice cream! There was a window by the table, and they could look down and see all the cars and the people. It was a happy day. I like _____."

---

12.   e. e. cummings, *Complete Poems 1913-1962* (New York: Harcourt Brace Jovanovich, Inc.). Reprinted by permission.

That's a dandy story for a *little* child. For variety, let the child tell the story. Or you start it, and let the child finish it, or let the child start it, and you finish it. Or retell for each other a favorite story that you have read together. Never tell a story that frightens a child, and do not abuse the storyteller's art by using stories to moralize or to teach lessons. Just enjoy stories as a fun thing to share. Sharing is a demonstration of love. And a child who daily experiences human love is then able to understand a little of what God's love is like.

Observe bedtime. Ritually. Story time may be a part of it. So may a time of talking quietly about the fun things we *did* today, or the lovely things we saw today, or even the problems we encountered today. (When my eldest was two, we always had such a moment when we "talked about what we did today."

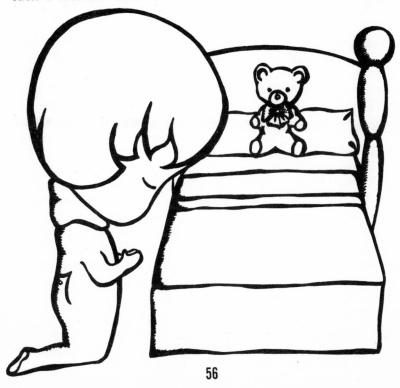

But I forgot one night, and tucked her in, and turned to leave. "Mama!" she called me back. And then, almost plaintively, "Talk we 'bout the did!" It mattered to her, and it was a custom we kept up for many years.)

Pray with her—with him—beyond the rote repetition of "Now I lay me ..." As you tuck your child in, each of you may alternately give thanks for the specific blessings of the day, and thus begin to establish the concept of prayer as a personal, simple, and sincere communication with God.

Write a letter. To God? Well—no—even though it often helps us think more clearly about what we believe to try to write it down. It would be misleading to allow the child to think that our communications with God need to go via the U.S. mail.

But writing a letter to grandmother can be an act of worship. Write it together. Let the child dictate part of it, with the adult as secretary to write it down. When the child asks, "What *else* can I say?" you may wish to mention the beautiful rain yesterday afternoon, or the good storybook you got from the library. And it may become appropriate to end the letter-writing project with a prayer of thanksgiving—for rain, and storybooks, and grandmother.

Read together. Introduce children early to the wonderful world of books. Even as toddlers they enjoy sitting beside you or on your lap, looking at and talking about the pictures. At first, it will be quite exciting enough just to "see the cat," and perhaps to share the fun of imitating what the cat says. Later they will enjoy the rhythm and the rhythmic repetition of "hundreds of cats, thousands of cats, millions and billions and trillions of cats," in Wanda Gag's book.

Until they are three, they will prefer books that have short stories built around everyday experiences. They will make friends with the characters they read about, and will see themselves doing the things the children in the story are doing. "It is something like looking in a mirror, only more fascinating." *Blueberries for Sal* is such a book. So is *Whistle for Willie.*

After three, they will be interested in adding books about the real world. *Mike Mulligan and His Steam Shovel,* for instance, or *Hello, Henry,* which presents an excellent "at home in the world" experience.

What has all this to do with worship? A great deal, if books are thoughtfully chosen. Overt examples are *Small Rain,* which is a collection of delightful illustrations to simple Bible verses, and Rachel Field's *Prayer for a Child.* But equally valid is *The Little Island,* which has a fine and rather subtle comment on the seasons, and another comment on faith.

Making Friends is a delightful (wordless!) book with a clear story line. *Sounds of a Summer Night, The Day We Saw the Sun Come Up,* and *Over and Over* are "secular" books, but each one does a beautiful job of setting the stage for worship.

In the Night is an excellent presentation of the friendly dark. *The Tenement Tree, Pussy Willow,* and *The Dear Friends* are all beautiful and memorable stories of the creatures in God's world. No child who has listened to a favorite grown-up read and reread *Pussy Willow* can be insensitive to spring.

The Happy Day celebrates spring's first flower. Sam celebrates the worth of the child who sometimes feels too little to count for anything.

When We Were Very Young and *Now We Are Six* are the Pooh-author's contributions to the younger set, and are as much fun to *read* as they are to listen to. So are some of the *Just So Stories.*

Millions of Cats is a just-for-fun book, and so are countless other books on the shelves of the nearest public library or book-mobile.

Go to the library with your child, early and often—regularly—to provide the wonderful enrichment of the world of books for *both* of you.

The library is a fascinating place. Enjoy it. Do not rush through, grabbing six books, any sort, and rush out again. But browse. Both of you. Most preschoolers want to pick out some of their own books. Splendid! Let them do so, even if they choose a book occasionally that is of little lasting interest to either of you. Just reserve the right to pick out two or three yourself. *You* can select *Sam,* or *The Tenement Tree.* Check out some you choose, and some the child chooses, and enjoy them all—some your child will want to check out again someday.

Then, read together, every day. Some families find this a good before-bedtime unwinding activity. Other families discover that evenings are too subject to interruption, and do their reading right after lunch, before naptime, or, when the child is a little older, in lieu of a nap. Whenever you do it, let it be a fun time. And perhaps more often than you would guess, you will see it evolve into a time of worship.

Read *When Jesus Was a Little Boy* to your children. Help them understand that once Jesus *was* a child, somewhat like themselves, who skinned his knees, and helped his mother with the chores, and who felt at home in God's world.

Go to church with your child. Let children participate in nursery and kindergarten church school classes. Let them enjoy being with the other children. Let them enjoy the teachers, who will enlarge their world, and the activities that will help them to express themselves as the people of God.

Expose children, through church suppers or family nights or other appropriate church experiences, to the *fellowship* of be-

lievers. Let them come to feel *at home in the church,* and friends with the people who go there.

Coming to feel *at home in the church* is a major and difficult accomplishment. Children will require some real understanding, on your part, of their point of view. They may not feel a bit at home in the sanctuary, for the pews don't fit, the songs are too difficult, and the sermon might as well have been in a foreign language. They may feel more at home in the nursery. If they do, let them have that good experience rather than forcing the issue and creating a bad one. But bring them into the sanctuary for *some* services you think they will enjoy. If your church has a Christmas candlelight service, attend it together. If one evening service features the older children putting on a simple play, make it a point to attend.

Or bring your children in for part of the service—the pretty organ music, some of the singing, the message to the children, if your minister presents one. Then take them back to the playroom for the remainder of the service.

Or, if you plan for children to remain with you during the full service, provide for their shorter-than-grownups interest span. Offer them pencils and small pads of paper when they begin to get restless. Let them hold your watch for a few minutes, and listen to it tick. Give them reassuring hugs. Offer them a hard candy to suck on. Bring along appropriate picturebooks to look at, that they may worship in their own way. Do whatever you can to make the experience a comfortable and happy one.

Enable children to participate more in the service of worship by helping them learn the Doxology, the Gloria Patri, the Lord's Prayer—or any other portions of ritual that might be used regularly in your own church. These can be practiced during the week, while you are sweeping the kitchen together, or riding in the car to the grocery store. To be able to say them with the rest of the congregation will make children feel quite big, and definitely *a part* of the gathered church.

Your children will be very much aware of the importance you place on church attendance. They *like* routine, and find in it a certain and satisfying security. When Sunday comes, they will assume that the family will go to church and will be ready for it, simply because it is Sunday. For many little children, going to church is the highlight of the week, and they will ask on Tuesday or Wednesday if it isn't Sunday yet.

Sometimes you go to a different church. This is a good experience, too, as the children become aware of a broader fellowship of believers. You may be visiting grandparents, or friends, and attend their church with them. Or you may be on a vacation trip, staying in the motel, and get up and dress and go to a strange church where you do not know anyone—simply because it is Sunday, and because it is your family's custom to join with others in worship. Jesus went to the synagogue "as was his custom." Your children, too, grow up with regularly repeated experiences of corporate worship. They learn at church that people *do* talk to God, that the Bible is an important book, that Jesus loves boys and girls.

Sometimes, though, you will *not* go to church. Jenny has the chicken pox, and must stay home, even though it is Sunday. The staying home provides a beautiful opportunity for planned family worship. The children will enjoy helping make the plans, and carrying them out. Shall we put a record on first? Shall we have a story? Shall we take turns saying a short prayer?

Perhaps we all need to remind ourselves that we can worship at home, too.

Give thanks at mealtime. Simply. Honestly. Avoid ecclesiastical jargon, but thank God instead for the good-smelling stew.

And receive graciously the *child's* prayer of thanks for ketchup. It is a valid and lovely prayer.

Some families hold hands around the table during the blessing. To do so may dramatize the symbolic family circle. To do so when guests are present may be a real way of saying "you are part of our circle." The simple gesture calls all to attentive listening while one (and not always the same one) expresses the common gratitude.

Table grace is no time for longwindedness, nor for a summarizing for God's benefit what has been going on all week, while the gravy gets cold. Certainly the long expository prayer, or one which sums it up vaguely with "We thank thee for thy manifold blessings" is not going to mean as much to the three- or four-year-old as the simple and sincere: "We thank you, God, for this food, and for the good, warm smell of the kitchen. And we thank you for our family. Amen."

Go around the table, occasionally, asking each person to name the thing for which he or she is especially thankful. (A pet turtle? It is the genuineness of the expression that makes it valid. And if the other kids laugh, that's okay, too. Shouldn't a prayer of thanksgiving be a happy affair, with a place for laughter? Perhaps we work too hard to get ourselves solemned-up for prayer.)

Sing the grace sometimes. Sing the Wesleyan grace to the tune of the Doxology:

> Be present at our table, Lord;
> Be here and everywhere adored;
> Thy creatures bless, and grant that we
> May feast in paradise with thee.

Or sing the Doxology. Or sing the old familiar Doxology words of praise to a new and jubilant tune. ("Jamica Farewell," for instance.)

Or simply *say* the thanks, in comfortable honesty. "Thank you, Lord, for this harum-scarum brood, and for all that they mean to us." Or, "Thank you, God, for ketchup."

Give thanks any time. Thank God for rain, for sun, for snow, for hot, growing days, and for the cold days of winter that give trees and bulbs a chance to rest. (You can't grow tulips in the tropics, you know.)

Thank God for Saturdays, when daddy is home from work—and for Mondays, that he has valid work to do. And for Sundays, when we may join with others to sing our praise.

Talk with your child. Mostly, moments of worship happen when you *talk* with your child. It is so easy *not* to, so easy to tune a child out, to let him—or her—ramble on and on, while your *own* mind decides what's for supper, makes a grocery list, or even starts composing a letter to the editor. But tuning a child out denies her the right of your mutual companionship. And it can become an insidious habit.

Mostly, moments of worship happen when you talk with your child about whatever you are doing or seeing or experiencing. Look at an artichoke in the grocery store. Even if one isn't on your shopping list, you can stop to admire the design, the composition, the symmetry. What God hath wrought!

Do not sermonize a child to death—but do rise to the occasion when one presents itself, and say whatever needs to be said to make the moment valid.

Sometimes it will be the child, not the parent, who does the articulating. What you think needs to be said is hard to say. You can't think of the words. It happened like that at our house the night our neighbor died. Mr. Primm, next door, was Julie's daddy, and Martha's—a kindly man who always had a cheery word or smile, even for small neighbors. And now, quite suddenly, Mr. Primm was dead. Becky and Doug lingered at the supper table after the older ones had left. "They are thinking about Mr. Primm," I surmised, "wishing they really understood what it was all about. They are feeling a little of the loneliness that must be almost overwhelming to his own children tonight. Maybe they feel a need to talk about it but don't know how to or whether to bring it up."

I didn't know how to or whether to, either. What can one say about the death of a good man, to a child who is barely six, and another who is almost five? But still they sat there, gazing with unseeing eyes at the pictures on the backs of the cereal boxes.

"Uh—," I began, thinking how eloquently I'd *like* to be able to say it. "Mr. Primm is dead. We are sorry, for Julie and Martha will miss him. We will miss him, too. He was a good neighbor. But there is something for us to remember at times like this— that death is as much a part of life as birth. It is just as natural, just as much a part of God's plan. And God who loved Mr. Primm when he lived next door still loves and cares for him, and still loves and cares for his family."

Becky nodded gravely, her eyes wide with the intuitive wisdom that children sometimes reveal. "I know," she said. "The preacher came to our Sunday school class last Sunday, and we talked about it. He said it's like a cocoon."

Doug looked up with interest. Cocoons he could understand.

Becky went on. "A cocoon looks all dead. In a way it *is* dead, because it is shut off from the world that it used to know. Then one day. . . ." Becky paused, her eyes mirroring the delight of the vision she described. "One day, the cocoon opens up, and a beautiful butterfly comes out." Doug's eyes were bright, too. Butterflies were happy creatures, and he would wish happiness for his friend Mr. Primm.

I hugged Becky close for a moment, partly out of gratitude that she had expressed for me, in terms with which they could both come to grips, that which I had found so hard to say.

But Becky pulled loose. She wasn't through. She said, "You know, that caterpillar in the cocoon didn't know what it was going to be like, to be a butterfly. It didn't know how it would feel to fly. All it knew was that it had to spin that cocoon. So it did it."

She frowned, thinking of the unlovely creature settling down to a task it did not understand. "After it became a butterfly, it remembered what it was like before, but it didn't want to go back."

Oh Lord, God—I should explain the mysteries of life and death to these thy children? The simple trust of their faith explains many things to me.

It was truly a moment of worship. But it would not have happened for us if we had not *tried to put it into words.*

Read the Bible to your child. Do not make it a "taboo" book which is forbidden to touch, lest it be dropped or otherwise desecrated. Let your child come to regard it as a book to be *read,* to be sought out for the means of expressing deep feelings.

Turn to it, in moments of real joy, to find expression for that joy. Enjoy its poetry, the majesty of its expression. And let your child see you turn to the Bible as a source of inspiration.

Much of the Bible is, of course, beyond a child's comprehension. But some of its finest passages are among those which children, too, can appreciate and enjoy. So *read* from the Bible, selectively. Handle the Bible, and let your child handle it, too. Read the lovely spring poem from the Song of Solomon (2:11-13*b*).

Read "Thine is the day, thine also the night" from Psalm 74:16-17. And read the lilting praises of Psalm 150:1,3,6. Read Psalm 96:11-13a:

> Let the heavens be glad, and let the earth rejoice;
>> let the sea roar, and all that fills it;
>> let the field exult, and everything in it!
> Then shall all the trees of the wood sing for joy
>> before the Lord, for he comes.

When the child comes in some summer afternoon with an ant, caught in a can, or with a grasshopper, look up Proverbs 6:6-11, and Proverbs 30:25-28.

Read *"This* is the day...." (Psalm 118:24) and "Let the children come to me" (Matt. 19:14).

Read the Christmas story in Matthew and Luke.

Read Genesis 8:22, and James 1:18a; and the jubilant lines of the Second Isaiah: "They shall mount up with wings like eagles" (Isa. 40:31).

Read often and joyfully from the Psalms, and read from the simple Gospel account incidents in the life of Christ. Read from the Bible casually—that is, without adopting an ecclesiastical attitude or a pontifical tone of voice. Read from it regularly.

And occasionally articulate your thanks for the Bible. Talk casually about those who wrote it—those like Amos, who kept sheep, and took the wool to market; like David, who also kept sheep, and played a harp, but who became a king. Talk about their love for God.

Read to your child from a simplified Bible storybook. Mary Alice Jones's *Tell Me About Jesus* is one early one. Avoid for a while those collections which are still too old for your child. But help your child come to know about the characters in the Bible, and come to enjoy their stories.

When, in your own Bible reading, you come to a verse that seems particularly suitable for a child, share it.

That seems to be the key, all the way through: *Share* it. Share with your child your gratitude for the gift of life. Share your joy in the simple pleasures of every day. Share your faith in God, who created all this. For worship is not so much a schedule as it is an attitude. Let your attitude toward life reflect your faith, your feeling of being at home in God's world. And then there will be many ordinary things that you and the child can do or say together that can become experiences of worship.

Amen, Amen!

Bibliography

Brown, Margaret Wise. *Pussy Willow.* Racine, Wisconsin: Western, 1972.

Burton, Virginia Lee. *Mike Mulligan and His Steam Shovel.* Boston: Houghton-Mifflin, 1939.

Eberling, Georgia Moore. *When Jesus Was a Little Boy.* Chicago: Children's Press, 1954.

Field, Rachel. *Prayer for a Child.* New York: Macmillan, 1944.

Gag, Wanda. *Millions of Cats.* New York: Coward, 1928.

Garelick, Mary. *Sounds of a Summer Night.* New York: Young Scott, 1963.

Gay, Zhenya. *The Dear Friends.* New York: Harper & Row, 1959.

Goudey, Alice E. *The Day We Saw the Sun Come Up.* New York: Scribner's, 1961.

Horwich, Frances R. *The Magic of Bringing Up Your Child.* New York: McGraw-Hill, 1959.

Johnson, James Weldon. *God's Trombones.* New York: Viking Press, 1927.

Jones, Mary Alice. *Tell Me About Jesus.* Chicago: Rand McNally, 1944.

Keats, Ezra Jack. *Whistle for Willie.* New York: Viking Press, 1964.

Kipling, Rudyard. *Just So Stories.* New York: F. Watts, 1902.

Krauss, Ruth. *The Happy Day.* New York: Harper & Row, 1949.

Lederer, William and Burdick, Eugene. *The Ugly American.* New York: W. W. Norton, 1958.

McClosky, Robert. *Blueberries for Sal.* New York: Viking Press, 1948.

Milne, A. A. *Now We Are Six.* New York: Dutton, 1958.

_____. *When We Were Very Young.* New York: Dutton, 1924.

Scott, Ann Herbert. *Sam.* New York: McGraw-Hill, 1967.

Schulz, Charles. *two-by-fours.* New York: Warner Press, 1965.

Seredy, Kate. *The Tenement Tree.* New York: Viking Press, 1959.

Shick, Eleanor. *Making Friends.* New York: Macmillan, 1969.

Showers, Paul. *In the Night.* New York: Crowell, 1961.

Schweizer, Byrd Baylor. *One Small Blue Bead.* New York: Macmillan, 1964.

Vogel, Ilse Margaret. *Hello, Henry.* New York: Parents' Magazine Press, 1965.

Zolotow, Charlotte. *Over and Over.* New York: Harper & Row, 1957.